A Beginning-to-Read Book

Halloween

by Mary Lindeen

NORWOOD HOUSE PRESS

DEAR CAREGIVER,

The *Beginning to Read—Read and Discover* books provide emergent readers the opportunity to explore the world through nonfiction while building early reading skills. The text integrates both common sight words and content vocabulary. These key words are featured on lists provided at the back of the book to help your child expand his or her sight word recognition, which helps build reading fluency. The content words expand vocabulary and support comprehension.

Nonfiction text is any text that is factual. The Common Core State Standards call for an increase in the amount of informational text reading among students. The Standards aim to promote college and career readiness among students. Preparation for college and career endeavors requires proficiency in reading complex informational texts in a variety of content areas. You can help your child build a foundation by introducing nonfiction early. To further support the CCSS, you will find Reading Reinforcement activities at the back of the book that are aligned to these Standards.

Above all, the most important part of the reading experience is to have fun and enjoy it!

Sincerely,

Shannon Cannon

Shannon Cannon, Ph.D.
Literacy Consultant

Norwood House Press • P.O. Box 316598 • Chicago, Illinois 60631
For more information about Norwood House Press please visit our website at
www.norwoodhousepress.com or call 866-565-2900.
© 2016 Norwood House Press. Beginning-to-Read™ is a trademark of Norwood House Press.
All rights reserved. No part of this book may be reproduced or utilized in any form or by any
means without written permission from the publisher.

Editor: Judy Kentor Schmauss
Designer: Lindaanne Donohoe

Photo Credits:

Shutterstock, cover, 1, 3, 4-5, 6, 7, 8-9, 10-11, 12, 13, 14-15, 16-17, 18-19, 20-21,
24-25, 28-29; Dreamstime, 6 (©San32 and ©Urmoments), 26-27 (©Seanlockephotography);
iStock, 22-23

Library of Congress Cataloging-in-Publication Data
     Lindeen, Mary.
      Halloween / by Mary Lindeen.
         pages cm. – (A beginning to read book)
      Summary: "Learn about Halloween traditions and symbols, including carving pumpkins,
wearing costumes, going trick-or-treating, and more. This title includes reading activities
and a word list"– Provided by publisher.
      ISBN 978-1-59953-689-7 (library edition : alk. paper)
       ISBN 978-1-60357-774-8 (ebook)
      1. Halloween–Juvenile literature. I. Title.
      GT4965.L395 2015
      394.2646–dc23
                                                    2014047635

Manufactured in the United States of America in Stevens Point, Wisconsin. 275N–062015

October 31st
Halloween

Halloween is a special day in the fall.
It is always on the last day of October.

Look at this house!

It has lots of
Halloween
decorations!

Spiders, bats, and cats.

Witches, ghosts, and skeletons.

Halloween has lots of these!

Pumpkins are picked in the fall.

You see lots of pumpkins on Halloween.

You can use a pumpkin to make a jack o' lantern.

First you cut off the top.

Then you take out the seeds.

Next, you cut out the face.

Put a light in it.

Boo!

You can put
on a costume
for Halloween.

Some costumes
are silly.

Some costumes
are scary.

What will you be
for Halloween?

You can go to a
Halloween party.

You can go
trick-or-treating.

You can get treats
on Halloween.

Thank you!

Look at all these treats.

Happy Halloween!

CRAFT AND STRUCTURE

To check your child's understanding of this book, recreate the following diagram on a sheet of paper. Read the book with your child, and then help him or her fill in the diagram using what they learned. Work together to identify words or phrases from this book that tell about Halloween. Use them to complete the diagram.

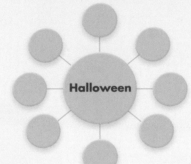

Halloween

VOCABULARY: Learning Content Words

Content words are words that are specific to a particular topic. All of the content words for this book can be found on page 32. Use some or all of these content words to complete one or more of the following activities:

- Create an idea web for the content words. Write a content word in the middle of the diagram. Help your child write related words and ideas in the outer circles.

- Ask your child to use his or her own words to define each of the content words. Have your child use each content word in a sentence.

- Help your child find content words from this book in other written materials in your home.

- Help your child make associations between two content words. Pick any two content words, and have your child think of something these words have in common.

- Have your child identify a content word by using three clues you provide; for example, *apartment*, *tent*, *cave*→*shelter*.

FOUNDATIONAL SKILLS: Long vowel sounds

A long vowel (*a, e, i, o, u*) is a vowel that sounds like its name (for example, *a* in *name* or *o* in *home*). Have your child identify the words with long vowel sounds in the list below. Then help your child find words with long vowel sounds in this book.

fall/face	top/treat	go/get
light/lots	ghost/get	these/this
seeds/special	trick/time	bats/be

CLOSE READING OF INFORMATIONAL TEXT

Close reading helps children comprehend text. It includes reading a text, discussing it with others, and answering questions about it. Use these questions to discuss this book with your child:

- On which day in October does Halloween fall?

- What is a jack o' lantern?

- What are two scary costumes to dress up in?

- What are two silly costumes to dress up in?

- Why might you put a candle in a jack o' lantern?

- What do you think is the most important thing about Halloween?

FLUENCY

Fluency is the ability to read accurately with speed and expression. Help your child practice fluency by using one or more of the following activities:

- Reread this book to your child at least two times while he or she uses a finger to track each word as you read it.

- Read the first sentence aloud. Then have your child reread the sentence with you. Continue until you have finished this book.

- Ask your child to read aloud the words they know on each page of this book. (Your child will learn additional words with subsequent readings.)

- Have your child practice reading this book several times to improve accuracy, rate, and expression.

••• Word List •••

Halloween uses the 69 words listed below. *High-frequency* words are those words that are used most often in the English language. They are sometimes referred to as sight words because children need to learn to recognize them automatically when they read. *Content words* are any words specific to a particular topic. Regular practice reading these words will enhance your child's ability to read with greater fluency and comprehension.

High-Frequency Words

a	day	is	on	then
all	first	it	or	these
always	for	last	out	this
and	get	look	put	to
are	go	make	see	use
at	has	next	some	what
be	house	of	take	will
can	in	off	the	you

Content Words

bats	face	light	scary	thank
boo	fall	lots	seeds	top
cats	ghosts	October	silly	treat(ing,
costume(s)	Halloween	party	skeletons	trick
cut	happy	picked	special	witches
decorations	jack o' lantern	pumpkin(s)	spiders	

••• About the Author

Mary Lindeen is a writer, editor, parent, and former elementary school teacher. She has written more than 100 books for children and edited many more. She specializes in early literacy instruction and books for young readers, especially nonfiction.

••• About the Advisor

Dr. Shannon Cannon is a teacher educator in the School of Education at UC Davis, where she also earned her Ph.D. in Language, Literacy, and Culture. She serves on the clinical faculty, supervising pre-service teachers and teaching elementary methods courses in reading, effective teaching, and teacher action research.